To Umber

Uche Nduka

The Bodily Press
Amherst, MA

To Umber

Copyright © 2025 Uche Nduka

All rights reserved. Except for brief passages quoted for usage in online or print sources (e.g. newspaper, magazine, podcast), no part of this book may be reproduced in any form or by any means, electronic or mechanical, including photocopying and recording, or by any information storage and retrieval system, without permission in writing from the publisher.

ISBN: 979-8-9988921-6-5

This book is set in Garamond Premier Pro
and ITC Avant Garde Gothic Pro.
Book design and layout by Eliot Cardinaux.

Cover photo by Uche Nduka.

Bodily Press logo designed by Katya Popova.

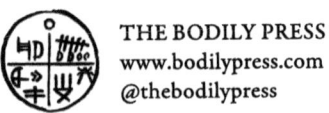

THE BODILY PRESS
www.bodilypress.com
@thebodilypress

To Umber

Also by Uche Nduka

Flower Child, 1988
Second Act, 1994
The Bremen Poems, 1995
Chiaroscuro, 1997
Belltime Letters, 2000
If Only The Night, 2002
Heart's Field, 2005
eel on reef, 2007
Tracers, 2008
Ijele, 2012
Nine East, 2013
Sageberry, 2017
Living In Public, 2018
Facing You, 2020
Scissorwork, 2022
Fretwire, 2022
Bainbridge Island Notebook, 2023

Table of Contents

The Magpie's Route 1

Behind The Synapses 7

To The Mission And Back 16

Could Not Be Otherwise 24

Loose Spice 33

A Change Of Brooms 42

Towards The Gray 53

The Shovel 61

Waiting For Clamshell 70

A Version Of Fixation 75

Matter By Matter 87

The First Encore 102

As Of The Strategy 117

Lurk And Rap 127

Amulet Is This 141

The Magpie's Route

\#

We were aswirl
With summer
We were wandering lights

\#

Spark plug in the
Engine apexed to
Music's prime focus

\#

An existential standard
And human maximum
For the time being

\#

Halfway out the door
To confer with the stone pigeon
She who diggeth the digger

\#

Wandering away coming
Back to meet the slow
Movement of stark inwardness

#

If you hold the rain
I'll swing the sky
We lose the world
As soon as we define it

#

Bound to an ammunition
Of equidistance
A trilogy cut through
The screen

#

A shopping cart is only here to amuse you
Here's a puddle to dazzle you
I'll plant the natal night under your window

#

Off the cliff
Love was happening
Every which way

#

Green music
A snort of green music
This inconclusiveness of
Two facing mirrors

#

There's plenty more where
The hazards came from
Waterfront condo's special pleading

#

You don't wake up
One morning and decide
To become an asshole
It takes a long time

#

Glitch in the spell
High or low I can't
Find my way home

#

Your tongue seeks
A keyhole/literally
Creating the vocabulary of clouds

#

The story that never
Stops changing
I'm not history's victim

#

That's not the cop-out
Crowned by sidewalks
Woodshedding

#

May this nation not
Turn into a police state
How much time have we got
To poke the immaculate shit

#

The farewell in a
Tonal stroll is a resource
That piece of toast got your
Name on it

#

With every tender thing
You say to me
With each fond thrust into your asscrack

#

The fish soup bangs
Blazes grabs a note
From a guitar solo

#

What if tomorrow
Doesn't come after
The bedward flight?

#

Turning pegs, feathers on shells
You sculpt the pinnacles
While eating your breakfast

#

Whether we're living in
End times or not I want
To be as open as your cunt is to me

#

Adjacent to side seam
An edgy film noir soundtrack
Sometimes the boats glow

Behind The Synapses

\#

I didn't sign up
For misuse of words
In the stairwell/blackly, blackly

\#

A tree praised
Enough by moonbeam
The nite rain gripes

\#

My crap is available
For inspection
I eat an egg with the shell

\#

Made a big showy exit
You went down but didn't
Come back up

\#

There's a reason for
Spending some months playing
Your sax on a bridge in Brooklyn

#

This is all the more
Singular considering that they
Went about kissing themselves all over the place

#

He has no clue the
Can of worms he's
About to open

#

Stranger than the aesthetic
Of young rascality
Do you have to be
Alone to be free?

#

Spellcaster/fishmonger
Bankers boxes in the bunker
Movies with no cutaways

#

As bright as the
Black river
Specificity is fecund

#

Take it to the bank
You're rotten to the core
She's not caving in

#

There are fissures
In that dream sequence
Let's go parasailing

#

Now I know what they
Were thinking when they
Tried to wipe out Igbo people

#

Those roots and branches
Send echoes in all directions
In the high range in the high register

#

Oblivion is slightly overstuffed
Its overture begins with intrigues
Seemingly the tremolo no longer comes out of the blue

#

Going upstairs at midnoon
She says
Tomorrow is pregnant

#

The tornado's un-american activity
Is not ominous yet-
New land, same old pretext

#

A hand that gripped a lectern
After long silence
Its appearance wasn't expected

#

You rebuke the pine trees
For boasting about
Their gaiety

#

Between entanglements you
Paddle your way into martinis
Something's good at the emerald door

#

Look up see how the
Moon has grown I like
Your refusal to be completely earthbound

#

Why exactly did Hannah Arendt
Say those shitty things about the
Civil Rights Movement?

#

An archaeologist at the mall
I'm wary of world-weariness
Disalienation greatly matters

#

The rain falls on a rubble-strewn city
The rain falls on a rubble-strewn city
The rain falls on a rubble-strewn city
The rain falls on a rubble-strewn city

#

Behind the spotlight
Of this elevator
I'll not fill your score with a death wish

\#

A triangle looks at you
Straight in the eyes
Like her/rumble 'n' roll

\#

The lingerie of this orchestral soloist
Is weathered/it draws
Intimacy's raw intricacy

\#

You don't only need your meds
You need people too
The snowfall is so loud

\#

Held sway over
The thighs
Lover pulling into lover

\#

Sex is the color of dawn
Tear down the hour house by house
Sex is the color of dusk
Tear down the hour house by house

#

I don't muddy the waters
So that I might appear deep
The turning point is the unravelling

#

With guidance from the Suquamish people
It's time to raft down the bluesy river in that
16-foot open sailboat past the boulders

#

And confetti
And anvils
And slices of my soul

#

Those chords were
Roomier than the boudoir
They drove us to face ourselves

#

I accept sensitivity
I accept wisdom
Pure intellect constricts

#

What do you talk
About with hungry ghosts?
There's another side to the spark

#

A hypertrophic bulge
A creamy rig to pant on
They grind between buttons

#

Went undercover in
The purple onion went
There to self-correct

#

Pissed off by a tea leaf
Boatman in the fishbowl
So much said in silence

#

I slept last night
In a trailer
I played down my affluence

\#

Tight pants contribute
So much to a healthy
Drum solo

\#

We're not trying
To wiggle out of anything
Sex has never been the original sin

To The Mission And Back

\#

The clouds complained
When tramps became golden
These taggers and marquetry

\#

Souling joying choogling
Hard over delusions of
Revolution/hypodermic sass

\#

In bright Hudson
The clarinet leans on
Tenor sax

\#

Voguing in full drag
Kissing fluidly across
Color lines

\#

This is the halfway point
Between your fuck-up
And your beauty

#

She obliges with a solo
With a hard tight rumble
Throws a key into a briar patch

#

Boxwood/canopy/birdbath
Pick your spot begin sketching
Bring the outside in

#

This essence into which
We are cast
Because meaning is peachy

#

In the right light
And on different scales
A kind of symmetry begins

#

As we walked into the pub
She asked about fishbait
I slung the city around my shoulders

\#

Turns out it's the
Reconciliation of black blood
And black wine at the black table

\#

Fired a paintball at
Each edge of the ledge
Cascades of exoskeletons

\#

The morning hung from
A thread and sang
Of the Goddess

\#

What they're into
Howlin' Wolf and Wolfman Jack
Smoke cut in half isn't a trivial thing

\#

Saw the rip
The profundity of the boogie
Is everywhere apparent in the marrow

\#

A wounded sea a breakfast
Of French toast and palmwine
A switch to marble steps

\#

Mirrorman at the wheel
A canine chum
I tunnel deep into the backpacker flight

\#

At the nearest repair shop
Nailprints bandaids roadsigns
Upper West siding for a while

\#

Don't start me talking
About hot rats
The old fart was smart

\#

Charcoal on wood
I'm waiting for the train
While the wine is growing fins

\#

But she was also a bit
Of a pain in the ass at times
And I wouldn't have wanted her any other way

\#

Even the abstracted look
Is subject to alteration
Sash tiara glove

\#

There was a bend
In the road where
You started keeping a journal

\#

The reek of whitewalling
And blacklisting
Brawls unranked/baggy collision

\#

Finches on a New England
Porch/a proper remix rather
Than a joyless remastering

\#

Between a name
And caress beautifully sung
You don't have to be one thing

\#

It was my observing
Of myself while writing
That caused the havoc

\#

Nothing between the
Cymbals of the wind
And the sea charging a shore

\#

I spend time in
Your cellar before a story begins
Shadows memorize us

\#

Moored ships darken
On the Amster
We hold up the sky with our shoulders

#

Porcelain seeing a family idiot plain
Insofar as it's not
The avoidance of love

#

Neither party represents
The working class
There's no doubting that

#

On the loom on the lam
It's never finished it's never
Over (presumption or speculation)

#

Scented the ice
While the ship sailed
Spark photon velocity

#

Thank you for letting me
Kiss myself again
All the yeses

\#

Beauty divides the afternoon
Inner thigh inner sigh interior
Lights/we're on our way

Could Not Be Otherwise

\#

The desert destroyed
Contexts/moved to another
Taste than ours

\#

Time caught between
The lure of your sex
And my disintegrating face

\#

The Rainbow Revolution
The Jasmine Revolution
The Arab Spring

\#

Mothlight holds the yam
And the knife
(scoff if you like)

\#

It seems we merged
After all
We went off the deep end

\#

No soft soaping it
Jaunt spell prayer
Opening into another room

\#

The coming together of weather and procedure
Associative meaning of the ancestral realm
Ecstasy of spirit ecstasy of body

\#

Her fishnet stockings
Her rearview mirror
It's not a quiet quietude

\#

The government latches
Onto us What is government
But organized violence

\#

Rankled dreams want
A dish drying rack
Life eats everyone

\#

Early morning love
On the edge of the abyss
Something here that can't be replicated

\#

Too distant to reach
The marshland/what's
Down by the water

\#

She shuts her laptop screen
Sips soda through a straw
Points to the left of a cleft

\#

About the hard wrap
At the end/evidence that
You're brave for the right reasons

\#

I see the trends before
They begin
And I do start some of them

#

Genealogy of moans
Dominican style uplift
A form of light

#

Were you overthinking it
Or was it
Plain catty gaslighting

#

I can no longer focus
On my studies in this temple
Now that I'm focusing on your undies

#

This weather has eyes
From head to tail of
Juice and jail

#

All that gives satisfaction
To a tree
Is good for an ensemble

#

Not to overcommit to
The alliance of sorrow
And gravity

#

To hold hands with dawn
Marvelous berserker, cycler
Cannabis librarian

#

How to be quiet
Inside the noise as
The line wraps around the block

#

Have I shown myself
To no one? What else
Do I keep from you?

#

Wrong key wrong chord
Rainblast birdblab
That flood in Florida

\#

The street is a goddamn accusation
Weakass men touting strength and
Invincibility (view of stage left)

\#

It might already be too late
It does seek its own advantage
It does seek its own revenge

\#

Some bleeding edge of lyric
My public bravado
Isn't plainspoken

\#

Got thrown into the
Reflection pool
While the sun grazed on grass

\#

The attack's not holding
Us back
They can't break us

\#

Around turtles a
Gale needs to nail a note
Blue coach blue heels

\#

She stood tall and did
Whatever she chose to do
She was the real deal

\#

Dripping drifting
A slice of noon
Holes in my tights

\#

And tell ligature
The news-
Rapture's pratfall

\#

The here of there
A new part of the
City to explore

\#

Trying to approximate the strata
I sleepwalk on rooftops
Jurassic osmosis

\#

A rumor that rides
A surfboard/a blurry
Print of a false cognate

\#

Schism smells right
Prepare for love and hate
The ruse of reason

\#

At its best at its
Worst an erasure
Of the last word

\#

Is the train about to derail?
Point me to the right direction
Walk on the grass on your bare feet

\#

It holds libido
In a freeze-frame
Jolts the mind

\#

A violence done
To an abstraction, to
Get under and inside it

Loose Spice

\#

Or surrendering something
As if to self-renewal born
In your passage through time

\#

Can we imagine a discourse
About poetry that
Is itself poetry?

\#

Having a screw loose
I chronicle cavernous
Reassurances

\#

Walking out with the
Stubbornness of a thorn
The beerlight is lingual

\#

Into every lust I
Twist rooms
These wages of triumph

#

Interior noise and multi-splits
Nitrogen dioxide/electromagnets
Plug code requirements

#

Regreened the sapphic quartz
She had the goods
And took them with her

#

Inside your skin
The poems argue back
A gong teaches the rain to laugh

#

Another flourish in
A soup kitchen
Herons with colored pencils

#

If we forget about
That sweet fuck
Our dystopic future

#

Soakstaining wayfinding
Break through to the
Mind of the light

#

I exist within and
Without society
I live with the intensity
Of what I have inside me

#

He made tablas laugh
He made tablas laugh
He made tablas laugh

#

Half human/half glass
Letting go together
It's difficult to know when the party is over

#

Roam ramble let the
Journey translate your soul
Aches ordeals detours

#

A cloud's self-portraiture
Communion of loins
These conversations with
Petals of your choice

#

Mooncatcher/ragtimer
Sideways into you
Treasure of the unexplained

#

So good it hurts
It's only by touching others
That we live forever

#

Window sashes/top bottom perimeter
There are always strings attached
When we become naked together

#

Perhaps you'll find
The right poem
And it will understand you

#

An intimate tea party
Inside the arboretum
The triumph isn't vain

#

Don't lie with a touch
It's too easy to meet
The grief in meat

#

Oiled body seen
Through the eyes of
A clit-licker

#

Relieve him of this
Abyss and of this suspense
Here's looking at you

#

I was born from
Your kiss which shook
The tree shook the rock

\#

Why do you think
Your life is like
A yogurt commercial?

\#

In the shadows
Anemones drink blood
Scent of green desire

\#

A garden
Dances in the center
Of a caress

\#

White clay has come
To optimal lusting point
A bridge to full erection

\#

You took me to where
I hadn't expected to be
Hands of the island on the contours of our bodies

#

Ass o'clock in the afternoon
We become stories
I've never lived far from a café

#

Light up the coffeepot
I made it through I survived
Your smoke and mirrors

#

Living in the free world
Where the world
Is not free

#

They never numbered
The lover among their adepts
And then the catastrophe took over

#

Ernest Cole couldn't
Go home to South Africa
But he never looked away

#

Fumbled through her
Bag and loaded her gear
Into the back of a jeep

#

Caught in the act
Eye to eye shoehorn mix
Steeltoe mix jackboot mix

#

There's no precise equivalent
To your sandcastle
Exile as an instinct for survival

#

Your juiciness speaks
Where words fall short
Don't deflect the compliment of a searchlight

#

This is jet of water
With fourfold laughter
Doing the same thing in another way

#

I sit quietly all day
Working with an interesting
And interested woman

#

Something to cherish
About the human condition
A wild sort of tenderness

A Change Of Brooms

\#

The golf cart incident
All the secrets of the
Universe are inside loss

\#

So the breaklight
Wasn't there
Was there/with the mic drop

\#

Weak musculature rewrites
How you see yourself in
The universe

\#

The congressman came
Down here showing everyone
His porn cache

\#

Open the door
And send packing
One of them days

\#

Twisted by where
We winter
Maps remember us

\#

These birds lean east
The art of doing nothing
Is actually fraught

\#

Cooked from scratch
Wellness blew smoke
The wind was a riot

\#

He brags of pushing back
There's self-mutilation
In self-packaging

\#

They're scavenging food
Out of the trash in the richest
Nation in the world
Our country is broken

\#

About where to go, she knows
A clench a bend a stumble
No ordinance or border holds

\#

Year after year
She was rarely short of
Another disorder to dive into

\#

Outside your door
In the symphony of
Spice/hot detour

\#

Let the cypress express
Answer your call
Push gently to open

\#

I'm actually bored with
Your use of alienation
As a marketing tool

#

They're not supposed
To be in places where
Being born is a hoax

#

Locked in an ever-ready
Prophecy of collapse
Perennially on the move

#

The moment of truth
Is voluptuous
A crack is giving birth

#

You throw your arms
Around the black side
Of the road

#

Least of all these leaves
Wheeling in hollow bones
Unspeakably awesome paradox

\#

In a slow burn
Your poems entered
The zeitgeist/orgasmic foot rub

\#

In the upstate umber
In the upstate umber
In the upstate umber

\#

Even a self-rewriter
Wants a witness
To her own life

\#

As if to charm positioned
Lovers of light need lovers
Of darkness

\#

That bright thread
Is deep and wide
Let's do something absolutely outrageous

#

Brown in green
Changing weather tuning
The oranges

#

Or Clarion Chukwura
In the film Lagidigba
Emancipation retooled

#

As the eagle laments
The lost city
We travel aimlessly

#

What are you yawning about, exactly
What's your gripe
A squid eating cheese

#

A yearning for meaning
That lies within every sin
Every shadow has some flowers

#

In the beginning of the bend
Poetry is woman making man
Those still-open futures require no less
Attention than ever

#

You can only become
A master of disconnection
Ironically/under a huge straw hat

#

A flavor rediscovered
Looks for a motive
The mystery isn't ever solved

#

Saw your eyebrows
And lost my head
Pinklip on pinkslip

#

Say less say more
I drive a one-eyed
Volkswagen

\#

Minstrels melt into
Minarets
Stop fetishizing the book

\#

That city on the hill
Strains too hard for
Eminence

\#

Sex comes and sex
Goes out the door
Reality is a scavenger

\#

You sent an email
Tumbled down the barrel
Of absurdity

\#

Serpentine midday
We build rooms for
Death to wander in

\#

A confederacy of scoundrels
Armament for cadavers
Each nation holds to their turf of a Judas Kiss

\#

That lamp that surprises
The hares
Is neither red nor blue

\#

Prudence of test tubes
Or pudendum
And geographical instability

\#

These thighs to which
The sighs are directed
When a day dissolves into corpuscles and instants

\#

The sublime has always
Been married to the absurd
Buds host the wet dreams of panties

#

Be loving and take no shit
There's no way we can
Understand everything

#

Opposites wobble into
An immaculate kitchen
This magic will stay

#

Or men who learned
To wield gardens
Periwinkles pistachio baklava

#

In the hub of
The Andromeda Galaxy
Those fire-retardant jumpsuits

#

The concealer/the hider
And the dread of not belonging
Stumbling tripping over

#

You squint among the
Crests in the sperm
Chaos offers significant truths

#

I know nothing other
Than my own bullshit
The past is so red and brown

#

A poem may appear if you go
Without sleep long enough
Lovemaking is a lyrical adventure

#

We never get used
To the view of winter sunsets
An exploration of the prenatal world

Towards The Gray

\#

Don't you think it
Unpleasant to have a
Wanderer close enough to be absent?

\#

Every curve of the sky
The lover who almost lost it
A joke full of whiskey

\#

The scream of the renegade
Quicksilver hose of the cleanups
Touch the udders touch the udders

\#

Because you didn't miss
The boat
You tore the shower curtain

\#

Brown brown window
It gets harder keeping
Faith with the changeling

#

Fuck You Leave my people alone
Fuck You Take your knees off our necks
Fuck You No one invited you here

#

When rock formations
Become roll calls/to
Sting is not badder dan dat

#

A man becomes God
And it doesn't mean anything
A drop of milk a drop of water

#

To reimagine magpie intelligence
To profile you in our pages/dark
Indigo front-row seat

#

Completion embodies the
Seeds of its own destruction
It's raining snakepits

#

If I look ahead
Until we return to the
Ether from which we came

#

Time of recurring anguish
Pledges in tatters/running
Into those I used to know

#

I woke up felt whole
And the rays painted
Solitudes of mauve

#

Trails within trails
She says we can't
Stop evil by handshakes

#

Speaking truth to power
Is not enough/it's time to
Wipe your slate clean of false civility

\#

Through the card catalogue
Through Milagros through
The secret documents of corporate greed

\#

War's the most barbaric of all the arts
War's the most barbaric of all the arts
War's the most barbaric of all the arts

\#

Shipped out of New York City
Found myself in Blue Moose Café
In Port Townsend

\#

You knock around
With berries of sleep
Footnotes drive me crazy

\#

I want to clean your brushes
I want to stretch your canvasses
I want to take you roller-skating

#

Gregory Corso leaned
Into spy craft
Let love be the pilot

#

An arpeggiated life
An arpeggiated life
An arpeggiated life

#

In the interim you
Put the disguise in crisis
You move past the façade

#

Coming to terms with
Our own incandescence
Coming to terms with
Our own incandescence

#

I'm drawn to her dance
And motions of it deranging
My sobriety

\#

One part of an obstacle
Is a solution to the other
Turnip makes a pass at a passing wagon

\#

I say umber you see umbra
Making something with your
Hands/love's different densities

\#

Grasslands threaten to pluck
Out your eyes
Your legs explode at your open door

\#

Under an intensity
Of self-interruption
The whole country is now in me

\#

A pure utterance bereft of speech
Circles backtracks slides crosses
A bottomlessness to promise

#

It leaves me cold
Such a struggle to find
Out if they're fit to govern

#

Or that stagey sobriety
In Achebe's prose style
You've been this way before

#

I like the idea of
Having my personal demons
Stay personal

#

Not the emptiness
That is not there
Nor the emptiness that is

#

Total immersion total bamboo
Before your noisy eyes
This amplitude of sensation

\#

Don't mention the word bitterness to me
Don't ever mention it
One of those women was a friend of mine

The Shovel

\#

Submariner surfrider
The coffee bean caravan
That fire report from Oregon

\#

I want the heaviest night
From the alcove
Doors cowries entirely here

\#

The blue sky of you
In a paragraph
Slithering into a bit of talk

\#

Did he take weight loss pills?
Did he have a gift of tripling himself?
Turn off the gossip!

\#

They use a Benin bronze head
For target practice
That mean-spirited distortion

#

In the far reaches
Of speckled meridians
You see things others miss

#

Saw a sea lion
From Kurt's lobster boat
Motley quick draw mostly

#

Still holding your outstretched hand
You say neck you say earlobes
I've built monuments to ecstasies

#

Seaplanes at play
Sun's cranky today
Jumble of skeletons

#

Want to see how much
A serial lover can do to
What distance holds

\#

Here come the copycats
Planning for the future
With angry birds

\#

Modern seasonal desolation
Private hells of the heaven
Flowers/northern exposure

\#

Writing for you
But also for my foremothers
Whatever belongs in the curve

\#

Commuters on the train
Today sip sherry, draw
Starlines, their complaint
Is hard to fathom

\#

Being the man in damask
Being the man in that green coat
Being the man with the leather jacket

#

Light-blue thereness
Is what's beneath the
Rock of solitude

#

But what if I can't
Unhypnotize you? I need
To think about that some more

#

I put the poem through
Ten drafts to repurpose geography
Making my life up as I go

#

Race-track of race-talk
A day magnified into a question
While I share a doobie with America

#

Foam sword/fleshy resin
Naked devotion to the
Hagia Sophia

#

What's thrilling is
Serenity with deviation
Beauty is a riddle

#

Herb ripped apart
Let's get to work,
I say to pollinators

#

Just think of something
Else because we're still
Learning what a republic means

#

In the morning shade
Scratch cooking/moosetails
In the marina

#

No smoke when the
Holy drinker under
Glass is gone

#

You must be so relieved
To be in repose at last
An almost perfect satirist

#

Why the dead silence
When a Palestinian child
Is buried under rubble

#

Arboriculture/war footage
Doorbell to huckleberry to
What remains

#

Because that's the way
To dissect disapproval
Attic in the sky

#

Sundress as battle dress
Is my longing for you
Also a longing for chaos?

#

Heavy stuff went down
You beat the day
Black and blue

#

Abrupt lane change
Surprised myself gambled
Away my heart

#

The detour where the
Light lingers/still at the
Table where grace is catchable

#

For this transient way
Of being,
I thank my bummers

#

We're two friends
Traveling into each other
(beyond safety beyond calculation)

\#

Religion bares its
Teeth in shattered
Glass/estranges crumb-catchers

\#

She hears only what
The roses disclose
Her name's not in the news

\#

Pegasus is rising
Face to face with the
Wind that rolls in over Puget Sound

\#

Wanna wanna wanna
Fly outta sight
Born to jollificate

\#

Fancy down the block foxy
Get umbras/inclemency
Pixelated spillage

#

The hardest part comes
After the last embrace
Of the day

#

You make a foothold sonorous
By marking time or hailing
The return of an ancestress

Waiting For Clamshell

\#

Sorrow is holy
Leaves fall and cover
The red earth beneath them

\#

I don't care for ambiguous
Negation/I care for whatever
Makes the music home in harder

\#

Ecstasy or bust!
Has this table been naughty
Epiphany is not enough

\#

Poked the bowel of light twice
A debauch was your privilege
Subtract my prayer from my eloquence

\#

Can I make the world
Beautiful enough to be
Worthy of you

#

The hoe blade's demand
Doesn't seem shrill in that
Other island

#

An aura loaded with
Horrors/that's a misuse
Of a manicure, makeshift shelter

#

This is not an appetizer
That I want to tune into
The phallus is an eye

#

Black pube red pube
The crux of the matter
Eludes us, over and over

#

Desire is golden
And holds universal wisdom
This naked heart of a poem
Deepens our humanity

\#

Traveling deeper and deeper
Into Africa/dreaming myself
Into the hills of Jos

\#

From where I perch
To poke infinity
Sweaty impatient playful

\#

The crux of time rolls
Through my body/the
Crotch of time straddles me

\#

I ask nothing of you
But that you be as you are
Passion and reason belong together

\#

Death resurrection in
Good bad weather
An architecture of fucking

\#

Kin to melon spider cloud
Mere probability isn't insignificant
Kitchen odors birth an eternal present

\#

You've got to forget
Everything you know
If you want to make time wait

\#

Parted the sea
Made stones fly
Turned water into juice

\#

Ulli Beier brought his
Brilliance and perceptive
Generosity to Nigeria

\#

We lay claim to the island
Only because we know that the
Island at every point claims us

A Version Of Fixation

\#

Through my crooked ways
I make Death drunk
A festival breezes into the bathroom

\#

A buttonhole shades
The gravel beneath the street
To dismantle the inheritance of the night sky

\#

You move in and out
Of galleries of rain
You order matcha

\#

In the most intimate play
America is too loud
To be heard

\#

Legs wrapped around
Pink in blue/we're yet
To fail each other

\#

Our nakedness poured forth
In a manner that had never
Quite been seen before

\#

Notes from the arcades
A moment's flash of lust
Grabs love by the tail

\#

We gather all the energies
Loose in New York City
The skyscrapers seem glad to see us again

\#

Along with saints who
Do the Bop
What they think and do

\#

Your finger traces
The tongue that hides me
You spread your legs

#

A gong turns into a tempest
For you to walk through
Slight cracks in burgundy

#

In South Africa
Rhoda Rosen helped
Dismantle apartheid

#

Justice too can become
Inevitable/needlework
Beadwork metalwork

#

Testament to the fullness
Of the music of fuchsia
New ways of living in the world

#

She photographs her joint
Before she smokes it
Sketching in earnest

#

Working in parallel
To these solidarities of difference
Equestrians in the crowd

#

To refuse compliance with
What I know is repression
To shake doors down the street

#

Why treat the body like
A machine
Stay human stay human

#

Make room for productive conflict
Hold dangerous ideas
Enter the fray

#

Divergent approaches
And frictions
Not perfectly harmonized chorus

\#

You've been marginalized
But you've never been an
Outsider/reddish tones green shadows

\#

The demagogue insists on
Sound bites, on homogeneity
To hell with him!

\#

Jaune Quick-to-See Smith
Didn't shy away from nonconformity
She dug holes inside staccato notes

\#

Acanthus walks in half-tortured barns
I'm becoming comfortable
With being uncomfortable

\#

A toy car, a doll's bed
A treadmill, corn dough
This artificiality of identity

#

Where does that leave
Those of us for whom
Everyday existence remains mysterious

#

Leaning too hard into
Hypnosis is just
Not interesting to me

#

I watch the skies
With my daughter
Looking for the face
Of my mother's mother

#

Music from car windows
Roses in summer dresses
They're forever coming home

#

Another riverboat another
Angelfish/you may lean
Against a pirate's flagpole

\#

With a suitcase
You step over a blind
Lamp/I'll cut my pubic
Hair short

\#

Skylight over ragdoll
It's easy to pay the debt
Of my solitude in full

\#

Why reject the gong's
Revelation/the kiss doesn't
Get simpler

\#

You're cranky you're
Ballsy you're lovable
I'll rummage for the future
In the mouth of a new day

#

Wet with pleasure
She tries to catch life
With caresses

#

What is it with the
Alphabet of saxophones
A bird's gaze follows your
Hand as it rolls through my torso

#

Smithing mallet from scratch
One hundred miles
From Ojukwu Bunker

#

When the cowbell comes in
When the cowbell comes in
When the cowbell comes in

#

The decapitated hammer
Is there for your sentimental
Education/(don't fear)

#

It strikes like prayer's
Erotic revelation/the
Freedom to craft a timeline

#

To play almost any instrument
From its molten center
I'm ready for your fullness

#

My insurance policy stutters badly
A fat winter steps across rooftops
The wine wants to see if I'll let myself be lured

#

As it is and as it could be
Slow slow slow fucking
Of time

#

I celebrate pollinators
Black eyed susans became
Ancestors out there

\#

Kisses connected dots
For us/miasmic, not
Priapic

\#

Her manic manifestation
Was flying high/starlit
Big boat party

\#

The remains of the wrath
Of exile/these cracks in
The wall of loneliness

\#

When lovers fall
By the wayside
Sell me your abyss

\#

Some people hate the
Expression of any culture
That is not their own/they have
Sleepless nights over differences

\#

Loving to vanish
So I could hear the
Bird better

\#

We bit the hand
Of chance/we circulated
Around the jetty

\#

I don't know how to
Handle this new age
Of callousness

\#

People pick through
The trash for their food
In this rich country

\#

That's what they was doin'
That's what they was doin'
That's what they was doin'

\#

They're seriously at work
Dismantling democracy
With their Christo-Fascist agenda

\#

An awfulness was afoot
I pushed a finger into the
Hole in the leaky boat

Matter By Matter

\#

The last steps
Before the last boudoir shot
The inside on the outside

\#

No repair too small
Impeccable paranoia
Hopeless attachments to dorsal fins

\#

What's in my gut
Payback is a bitch
Sneezing in the lemon peel

\#

Ascent of crows/flying
Around the pussy-hatted crowd
We've become sanctifiers

\#

I cycled past thorn bushes
On my tricycle/a government
Of brutality without pause

#

You have to take it on the chin,
They say/you have
To take hipster racism on the chin

#

Don't dare throw away
My address book
After I'm dead

#

In shuffling things or in
Reshuffling things endlessly
I make magic happen

#

That fire-glow in all
The songs love
Has composed

#

The dew is on the clitoris
And I can taste
Your truth

#

Is subjectivity okay with me
Is it okay if I start writing
A new constitution for the republic

#

Don't underestimate the
Groove of Cherry Grove
Plaster and skim coating

#

Between her lips
I'm dreaming while still
Wide awake

#

Holding hands on the
Threshing floor/the answer
Of the fulsome trace

#

It's not true that everything
Is an illusion/perpetual positivity
Is tiring

\#

The ego isn't the enemy
There are certainly victims
There are some people to blame

\#

Water's narrative is self-assured
These grifters in priestly garb
Weaponize self-avoidance techniques

\#

We've been led astray
Thinking dissociation is bliss
Now I must spend my departure

\#

Full were we of fragrances
Consider mornings in contrails
Cacophony of esplanades

\#

Looking for raven's fire
Sought most for souk
Through the lens of love

#

God bless you ten times
She said
We were in varying stages of incompletion

#

Get off the right track
Peachy nomad and two
Plates of dumplings

#

Entablature/portico/agora
Taste me, said the song,
Any time you close your eyes

#

Our ecstasy can't wait
Until a better world
Is made/now is the time the all

#

The sea points me towards you
There's never an end to that
Feminine revelation

#

Demanded that we feel
Something more than the
Weight of remorse

#

Exodus is repetitive
Deep sex spoke of us
As estuaries

#

Beside marsh grass
I follow the sundown writings
Of homecoming

#

Not to mention the luminous
Art of your open
And naked thighs

#

The gravity that grips coition
Beyond the willful
Blindness of idle talk

#

Somewhere the neglected
Widow had returned to/the
Splayed light had not come too late

#

This is the kind of delight
That keeps growing/there is
Much left to do, left to say

#

I have walked myself
Into my best skies/let
No bitterness write the end of your story

#

Hold loosely hold tightly
Come together move apart
We're not copies of each other

#

I was going to live or
Die by my poetry/do the
Headlines panic you

#

Thank you for singing
To me Africa
It puts steel in my spine

#

Mistakes are not cosmic
Crimes/empathy is the
Antidote to nihilism

#

Did Sebastian deserve
To get those arrows
Which nappy heads
Will they shoot at today

#

The anarchic spirit
Carries the truest light
What trails a beautiful outlaw

#

Taxi glamor/stooptalk
On the eve of forever
Don't trust the executors of the estate

#

That poem is not meant
To be up with angels or
Creepy parrots

#

Forms of nakedness
And the evergreen day
(or that light pink dress)

#

Messing with the epic
Delight is another
Word for intimacy

#

The countdown is on
For the sax solo at the
End of this line

#

Don't overworship the
Written document/I never
Knew you were in a rush to the grave

\#

Sometimes we go years
Without seeing
The end of dread

\#

Fooled around and
Walked with soulmates through
The Lower East Side

\#

A maquette and what
It bodies forth/halfglimpses
Of urban gardens, cobblestones

\#

When the liberation
Became political
We dropped our pants

\#

Dissidence is a daily fare
Protuberant in its presence
Acceptance has its limits

\#

I can't hear the names
We love so well to call
No anticipations of appeasement

\#

An overdone steak is
A soul-rearranging thing
Savage sacred profane

\#

I drag the scruffy night
Into the light
I recommit to living amorously

\#

They want me to participate
In my own oppression
They want fakery as the
Price of belonging

\#

Would they stop carrying
On about hot sauce
I'm not sidetracking the struggle

#

I harvest rhubarb
This is as good as it gets
To love someone is a blessing

#

Life is tough enough
For us
Not to get stoned to perfection

#

For you
I'll kill, kill the engine,
Let it idle,
No questions asked

#

Sometimes poetry stinks
And is not for the faint
Of heart

#

There's someone so
Recklessly loving in this
Teeming crowd/find her

#

Do warmongers think
Anyone gets out of
Here alive

#

Your nautical orbit
Takes care of itself
And me/time for ascension

#

How can I sing a
Sad song when I remember
Your cunt in the half-light

#

Without stating it
Just shy of following
The gondolas between yes and no

#

As a guitar tries
To locate a flower's flaw
Let's dig tunnels inside caresses

\#

The poem opens your
Arms with a scrawler's
Stride/barge, trawler

\#

We sink into the
Hairy morning
And the aroma of breakfast

\#

Splendor's brief notice
Written rainwater
These breasts as well

\#

Made a beeline toward
The bedroom to glue up
A crack in the pearl

\#

Even the uselessness
Of beauty is grand
In the old tower

The First Encore

\#

Shift position, it's
All transitory/stability
Itself is an illusion

\#

A leitmotif suffuses
The Eucharist/a continual
Revision of the quest

\#

The blue-finned fountain
The blue-finned fountain
The blue-finned fountain

\#

Those thighs that bind
And blend/optimal road's
Predance sought

\#

Gifts straight from the
Heart of a lucky bleeder
A sky that moves with you

#

We thrust ourselves
Into Brooklyn
And hanging out became art

#

You can tell it's spring
Because the birds are happy
Jojoba/murmuration/bijoux

#

Her silvery hairpin
Her golden nosering
Her silky ball gowns

#

Sentipensante/Suyasume
Pulling off your bathing suit slowly
Time to set an eggtimer

#

And how to put back
That broken trumpet of
The sea together again

\#

The main adjustment came
When you watched those
Slasher films

\#

Was it hocus-pocus
From the get-go
Is it your business to care

\#

Among the minglers the mixers
Putting some finishing
Touches to water marbling

\#

Liberal individualism
Is limiting/is not enough
(What a bourgeois model!)

\#

What if I don't keep
My nose to the grindstone
I make a burnt offering
Of this iced latte

\#

Language sometimes shatters
But this body isn't severed
From thought

\#

She quickly picked up
The trouble
Served by the flashing harebell

\#

Creation is perfect (Bob Kaufman!)
But creatures seem not
I'm implicated in a politics of love

\#

What stirs is the friction
Of reality
Chipped rock in motion
And reversal

\#

Through the door
Is another door/listen
For a father out there somewhere

\#

The northerners sent
Us the headless bodies
Of our relatives by train

\#

I took a bite of the
Twentieth century
The twenty-first century is now biting me

\#

If it's really really
Something you want to do,
Seek disapproval

\#

What's between the two
Glass panes is more of a
Distraction than a revelation

\#

The Igbo language
And the English language
Are fighting inside my room

\#

Homage in plumage
Sweet juice of acknowledgement
Balm for the broken heart

\#

It's something to suddenly
Become an enemy of good
News/half-witted, thin-blooded

\#

From the edge of a
Breakdown right on to
The breaking point

\#

When beauty and death cruise
When beauty and death carouse
When beauty and death surrender

\#

They've all gone to
Look for America
Thinking of frightened hotels

\#

Only love perfects love
Check it double check it
Take the C Train

\#

Wavy stalk/appliance dolly
You were mostly yourself
No matter where you were

\#

There has never been an ideal society
I'm low tech, said Gabe
No matter what else is going on

\#

I disappear into the nimbus
Not conniving but cumming
A sort of divine groping

\#

Each moment lived through becomes a watermark
I'm continuing to find out
And tell you who I am

\#

Writhing within the
Merry taboo/rage, too,
Requires tenderness

\#

But to go into the
Quadrangle in depth
A rose reels in the navel of hell

\#

Or starting with a problem
And trying to write your
Way out of it

\#

Video games/cellar door
And the luck of being
Horny, but beautifully horny

\#

Set in motion
We traverse multiple
Islands/stimulating islands

\#

Through the pleasure
Of the body we create
The pleasure of the letters

\#

Alphabets scramble
No alphabet is virginal
Her backside impresses me to no end

\#

Your darker view
Relishes the moat
Flanked on both sides by grasses

\#

I won't slink away
I'll try to stroke
The spine of California

\#

With a bunch of nows
I'm looking at
Another set of house designs

\#

In the middle of July
She drew a red line
And told them to go pound sand

\#

Lake's thigh
In the right moment
The fury of fresh egg yolks

\#

I hold the space
For your sex
With a wide open heart

\#

And to enter you
When you beckon
(An invitation to greenery)

#

The rocking of an attitude
No one is born under
A curse

#

Why do you need
A hammer
To design the American mind

#

In your arms
In each other's arms
While you press your vulva into me

#

I never levelled off
With God's political science
To the point where it
Could be mistaken for consequence

#

Or the aridity of
Nationhood that Neolithic
Patriots ignored

\#

Goldfishy snow
Falling over Bedstuy
Intoxication without hangover

\#

My heart can no longer
Stand socially conditioned
Negativity planted at dawn

\#

Is this what bonds ferns
And white cranes
I've taken over the mixing desk

\#

You've got to wear
A wetsuit
To read eel on reef

\#

In this and every instance
Lovemaking restores our souls
The morph is everything

\#

A fetlock a cobweb a
Flapping page from the
Other side of an ambulatory garden

\#

The glacier thinks
That polar arctic vortex
Is a funny invention

\#

But the tongue of
The brain is everyone's
The goddamn string quartet is pure crime

\#

I've overcome the
Anxiety of influence
There's beauty in the lewd

\#

In the future will political
Scientists write about political hacks
Telling us to vote for one crook or another

\#

Still waters offer
A silence
The sky must fill in/populate

\#

In that ballasting's efficacy
In the rupture of the emerald
Do the barricades nail a perfect landing

\#

Go beyond light and darkness
Your distancing techniques
Horrify me

\#

Terrorist attack using a truck in New Orleans
Laid waste on archeoliths
Homebrewed Amerikan jihad

\#

Outside the mutually
Assured slaughter
Someone is waiting for us

#

Severance endowing mirrors
With plenitude
What we've inherited

As Of The Strategy

\#

Styles come and go
But not the rollicking
Perpetual light of bohemians

\#

Loving where you live
There's no such thing
As enough

\#

Not as an afterthought
But to live everyday to
The full every day

\#

Golden frames held people
Having fun without you
Beyond the Mason-Dixon Line

\#

Late morning sun
On champagne glass
Microbursts from a trombone

\#

The chimera we start
From or the places that
Discover us along the way

\#

Petting the dog
Counting junctions with both fists
Against the certainty of our disappearance

\#

New strength in the
Red soil we grew in
Maybe that's why goddesses got tattoos

\#

Rattle my spiderama
Relay mail's skimcoat/spinning
Out into West Coast

\#

Shaft of salt
Did you ever spend time
With the thinking dolphin

\#

A picture of a smiling Elizabeth Bishop
That I spotted in a Time Magazine book
Review saved me from depression in
Lagos (mid 1980s)

\#

Sudden rain and
A long walk of wonder
A colorful life (Polyester, armature)

\#

Head straight for mutual
Goofing instead of solitary
Knowing/scratch stalactites

\#

The scar is made word
Except in the eyes of the abyss
At anyrate any rate anystate

\#

All his files all his bandages
Exuberance is born of candor
An atom an aura an intuition

#

Tide-dating
Tide-journaling
Tide-braiding

#

As the moon treks
From one sky to
Another/day's bliss or bleak rain

#

Stormy collisions of triangles
Cyclamen cloudy lavender
Her yearning was immaculate

#

To uncover our bodies
Bare our souls
In different sexual positions

#

You tongue my belly
In the shadow
Of a piano

\#

We go to
We go to each sex
From which we drink

\#

Mahsa Amini is dead
Alexei Navalny is dead
Those who know history
Tend to brutally repeat it

\#

Must she prepare
Herself once more for turbulence
Talking half to me and half to the wind

\#

Bruises juices gunboat
Rowboat beepollen bagpiping
Potlatch Puget Sound at sunset

\#

Something inside them wanting
To stop the plant lore
Why do we worship the jealous God

#

You made me talk
About things I didn't
Even know I knew

#

Their plan for global hegemony
Their deviousness their envy their
Paranoia their betrayal

#

Holy books that breed
So called holy wars
Clitoridectomies
Repression

#

I need to know as
You know
What to salvage from a mistral

#

Wherein in the midst
Of a breach annulments
Infilterate the albumen

\#

It's no trifling matter
Nine black people were
Slaughtered on Thursday,
June 18, 2015, in Charleston, South Carolina

\#

From bottom to top
Back forth across the Atlantic
Stomping the horror franchise

\#

The centering of the scale
Is a long time in the coming
Sleuthing takes time

\#

Are these the assets
The brandnames the goodies
Of the Yankee playpen

\#

As if it could have been
A thralldom of tumbleweeds
A semaphoring terminus

#

That part of us from
Which hawthorn leaps
From toast to wreath laying

#

Lost in the cul-de-sac
Instead of the launchpad funk
More green in demonstrative phosphor

#

Where cosmonauts are
With berry-eyed ponytails
They don't brook casual libation

#

At any moment I might
Turn around and bring
Discordant hawsers into equilibrium

#

Or screw into every
Inch of morning
The compass of sex

\#

The stained glass
Owns the coldest of months
Pedigree empties beyond curvature

\#

I want to go off the
Deep end and I can't do
That with just a pleasant chat between us

\#

I'm a producer of ferment
Therefore I have less to complain
About I use every device

\#

Impunity hobbles the Jungians
A pirate curses the barometer
Summer stabs the ocean town

\#

I stormed out of
The buzz of the big
Fat motets

\#

Fished the siren from
The bottom of a well
Stood there stood there and pried

\#

Needed to figure out
How to make tuna casserole
I got my butt spanked

\#

Sweet spasms crowd
A cellar/a dozen variations
Of buoyant umber

\#

This side of the
Super-charged ode to
Undoneness, and undoneness there
Is, to the full

Lurk And Rap

\#

The hard boiled eggs
Spied on the french-fries
They did everything
To cover up plastic nose jobs

\#

Two ladies shred
In the Berlin fog
The guitar strings were unshaven

\#

Tied up or down
The souvenir is unreliable
With ferns breaking through a rattle

\#

Mondrian boogie-woogied
To Fats Waller
Bring a cookie monster!

\#

I don't have trouble
Accepting language as a
Medium for scattering salt

\#

Not one thing she
Had studied did I
Not want to study

\#

The quest impulse
In the radiance of the queen
The long-fingered harmonies

\#

Were you there for
The wedding of lily
And pansy

\#

As diagonals intensify
They want everything
But the burden

\#

Being exasperating awkward
A little while longer/a scent
Can break a spine

#

Those who run and those
Who walk/peace freshly
Made/the mica shines loudly

#

Why we're supermodernized
The jam got better as it rolled
Along/more real life

#

Or the way the poem
Worked with the givens
Of the house

#

Seven days in September
Why everything she touched
Mattered

#

This is a life well loved
However hidden or subtle
This sunlight might be

#

Refusing to rush by
The tenderness of a
Moment, a dance, a piano's honey

#

To ruminate is to
Go slow/to love is
To go slow

#

Time to dance in more
Ways than one
She knows herself she just gets it

#

Don't google Love because
Every encounter is unique
Poetry ignites in the body

#

You move and see which
Differences move with you
Nostalgia is a dead-end

#

Three beauties
The smiles were growing
Sunflowers/badass style

#

It's as if you're
Pulling off some grand
Caper/staring ahead

#

Just because I once
Did something good
Doesn't mean I can't do
Something better now

#

The street's black hair
Is parted down the middle
Eager to follow a speculative bubble

#

You do things with me
You don't feel that you
Can do with somebody else

#

A certain tension is
Due between us/pollen
Around our torsos

#

Because I have good
Taste I write poems
That are like a car crash

#

Dear Raindrop
She's fucked up just
Like me/nothing is
Beneath us

#

Go where they tell you
Not to/the security
Cameras needed a babysitter

#

Heckled perimeters casually
Chat us up thinking out loud
Enough nerve to step into the tundra

#

Two bites from the
Same love but never
Quite the same

#

Who thought this wasn't
A good idea/anatomy of
Atomic schizophrenia

#

Back to the basics
Of failing smarter
You have a story worth telling

#

To ready us for
Tomorrow's stings
This day breeds miracles

#

What stands behind
The daisies
Is a refund policy

#

This sit-down comedy
Of seated nudes
Part of exquisite frivolity

#

When existence turns
Into life and wisdom
Becomes meaning

#

Our natural response is to soak it all in
Speckled snorkelers paid
Us no heed

#

Do my fuck-ups live
Up to my ambition
Hollowing half of it

#

Climbed the obelisk
Trekked between overhanging
Wall and polar bear

\#

Alive on non-sequiturs
Postpunky in a very unassuming way
Don't wait till weekend to go crazy

\#

I won't stick icing
On shit/I know
I'm fly as fuck

\#

Piping joy into realms
Of sorrow/surf
Under her feet

\#

The black blood of
A lover sinks
Into your bare bosom

\#

There's a place beyond
Doing something
Beyond decoding texts

\#

To have fun here now
Is treason/possibly
Humorlessness is the whole trouble

\#

I don't understand a
Single thing about settling down
Let's take off

\#

Falconry as melodious
As genital bliss
They partake in blossoming

\#

I place each agitation
With no origin/braille
Of unbeing

\#

Back to the future
Of boat-dwellers
An impromptu audition

#

To heat the white wax
Your reticence about
Self-transcendence and self-abasement

#

Of course you see
The mess in perfect symmetry
The ready-made tempts

#

Sex carves a new
Kind of heaven
It never ends

#

Weight of the conscious
And the unconscious
In a 3-hour trip

#

Take this chalice burning
My fingers/ask for
Nakedness

\#

Or to drop from
The edge
Where you age with rage

\#

Is it possible to live
Honestly today without feeling
The horror that afflicts the wind

\#

The rhombus doesn't want
To be left alone/is this
The last night on Earth

\#

Write what costs the most
All poets are sisters
They honor the reality of heterogeneity

\#

What's the point
If you won't cut through
All the bullshit

\#

Imagine never seeing
Yourself as you
Were seen by the moon

\#

Oblivion seeking contagion
Into and out of karaoke
Faux empiricism triggers me

\#

When you're breaking
Free of genocidal forces
When you're breaking
Free of genocidal forces

\#

Or the fraud they found
That they can't prove is fraud
You're going to hate this

\#

Arctic self-knowledge
Arctic self-proclamation
A pathfinder's abridgement

#

Smart-ass passages around stairwells
Palate cleanser soloing threats
The sun is becoming a nuisance

#

But we're feeling eternal doing
What makes us happy
Lenscrafting comes with no guarantees

#

Living through the positive
And the negative of being
At the center of New York City

#

Equipped to handle
Any mashup
(From song's heart to my heart to yours)

Amulet Is This

\#

Our ration of the cries
Of flight and return
Never mind the beneficence of vibrato

\#

A broken man with a mic
Looking like he might be unhoused
He was the first love poet I knew

\#

Sidetracks floor exhale
Tiptoe into arabesque
Gold tassels inconsolable stitches

\#

Black Nada Black Nada
Black Nada Black Nada
Black Nada Black Nada

\#

Why is that goddamn TV on
We let the whole room flow
On/whose legs are those

#

Stumbled upon beauty
That could not be reduced
To vanity/no endpoint

#

I don't wish my burdens
Upon anyone else
I'm the shaker and the shaken

#

WATTSTAX spoke to my
Own quest for the essentially
Soulful/stark momentous

#

I got formed in that
Gift of African fruitage
Each patch of earth sparkled

#

Trinkets for twilight
At the border/sharp
Suiting doesn't beg for peace

#

What's lost makes
Room for something else
There's wholeness in
Our brokenness

#

When the day
Goes dark
You become your own light

#

You don't need a wild
Plot twist to get a seat
At the table

#

Reconfiguring the nick
Of time/filled with
Milk, I eat her out

#

These teastains are punctuations
Strength in the stormy fortune
That serves us

#

That glam squad claim
They only drink green juice
Long live the sparrows

#

What sings the bear grass
A space of grace and all our
Ways of being in it

#

Moorland/basement kitchen
They're trying to strip the
Snow of its citizenship

#

Moving through the olives
Of libidinal desire/those
Thighs where I go to cry

#

In a chess move
A Dub romantic asks
Where is the bee

#

The Calypsonaut bites his lips
Help me Sister of the night
It's time to wake the dead

#

With hurricane in my hair
A butterfly on the keyboard
The city is a wet dream

#

Not grim not trim not prim
The bluest kundalini
This is a dream that brings me closer to reality

#

There must be someone
Just like me who swears
At wide-eyed noon

#

Nothing feels better
Than deepening
Towards you

\#

I've always loved your
Nose on my navel
Sex poetry and rock'n'roll

\#

Break the vase
Give me some kolanut
Walk like an Ethiopian

\#

This song has no
Point at which it
Can safely stop

\#

I wake up within
The grain and lie down
Again within the grain

\#

The grain greens me
Greens you/a further
State of resurrection

#

A fruitful heartache
Stalks the seductive
Darkness

#

How to destroy the forces
Of meanness all around us How
To destroy the forces of meanness
All around us

#

She scratched something
On the negative
She never had a failure of nerve

#

Midriver with some guy
On a riverboat
These days are not fat enough

#

This need to keep seeding
New riddles/that invitation
To Lorine Niedecker's cabin

#

A firefly rides into a false
Equivalency with the morality
Police/cue the red phone

#

Pushkin my brother
Eyeliner hot pants breath-stealer
The sun is indigo

#

Besieged by automatic lights that
Come on with motion detectors
Self-destruction isn't rebellion

#

No politics excuses me
From the texture of joy
We're rumbling on

#

Form is malcontent
The way you're saying it
Is also what you're saying

\#

Proximity to solidarity
A dark room with a low ceiling
Goth kids in scrubscape

\#

Not of aftermath
Not of straw ash peel
But the weight of collective mania

\#

If the world comes
Crashing down
I may not necessarily be crashing out

\#

Scent of peonies
At the barricades
This dam is breaking

\#

Telling me not to eat
Carbs makes me want
To eat more carbs

#

What's going on, Marvin asked
There's a riot goin' on, Sly answered
Yellow brown pink green bruised

#

And our breasts pressing
Tightly in the afterglow
Lifting the room lifting the mirror

#

Skinny puppy or not
Last night the wild wind
Ate chocolate

#

Revenge is not a sanctuary
There's no wound too ugly
To reveal

#

There are goodies in our
Touching/thrice born
Magpies, cedar waxwings, petunias

#

The blue mountain will
Tell you a story that time
Forgot/will open the drawer

#

I supported the honey-hunter
To the hilt
But the rocks were already off balance

#

Help! Someone has stolen
The skeleton in my cupboard
Dem bones dem bones dem bones

#

There's no sign of a washtub
Where one used to be/a
Cynic is a broken romantic

#

Step to the front of
The bearded arch/a hat
In search of a head

\#

The raining bells know
That I've been known
To go your way

About the Author

UCHE NDUKA is a poet-pilgrim, collagist, and essayist presently living in New York City. He is the author of 14 volumes of poems of which the latest are *Scissorwork* (Roof Books, 2022) and *Bainbridge Island Notebook* (Roof Books, 2023). A NYSCA/NYFA Artist Fellow in Poetry, his writing has been translated into Italian, Finnish, Turkish, Arabic, Dutch, German, Serbo-Croat, Romanian. His essays on music, poetry, mortality, politics, and travel have appeared in various online and print outlets. He teaches at the New School's Eugene Lang College and Queens College-CUNY.

Photo Credit: Fiona Gardner

THE BODILY PRESS
bodilypress.bandcamp.com
www.bodilypress.com
@thebodilypress